Hiking and Climbing
California's
Fourteeners

Stephen Porcella - Cameron Burns

CHOCKSTONE PRESS
Evergreen, Colorado

This book is dedicated to
Kerry and Mary Burns, and Robert and Yvonne Porcella.
Four people who took their children into the mountains and
showed them the wonder of the summits.

Front Cover Photo: Sunrise on Mt. Whitney.
Photo by Steve Porcella.
Back Cover Photo: A climber on the summit at
Starlight Peak.
Photo by Cameron Burns

CALIFORNIA'S FOURTEENERS
ISBN 1-57540-006-5

First published in 1991 by Palisades Press

THIS EDITION PUBLISHED AND DISTRIBUTED BY
Chockstone Press, Inc.
Post Office Box 3505
Evergreen, Colorado 80439

PRINTED IN THE UNITED STATES OF AMERICA

Any comments or suggestions regarding the contents of this book are
greatly appreciated.

CONTENTS

PREFACE

This guide book is the result of three years of collective work. During this time period we, the authors, climbed over 65 different routes on California's fourteen thousand foot peaks. These routes ranged from technical first ascents to established popular routes. In the process, we collected historical and modern route information for the production of a large, comprehensive book on the history of climbing California's highest peaks. It was during our climbs that we quickly became aware that many hikers and non-technical climbers were having trouble comprehending route descriptions in previously published guide books. We decided that a small, compact guide book aimed towards hikers and non-technical climbers was needed.

This guidebook would not have been possible without the help of Sandra Elliott Porcella. Her editorial work, knowledge of computers, and incredible attention to detail proved invaluable.

We would also like to thank the following people for their contributions to this guide book:

Lesley Gaunt of the Mt. Whitney Ranger Station, Howard Grice, John Louth and Keith Waterfall-all from the White Mountain Ranger Station, Leif Voeltz of the 5th Season, David Alt, Walt Borneman, Robin Ingraham, Neecer Waterbury, James Wilson of Wilson's East Side Sports, Marian Helling, Keith Osborne, John Caratti, Burton and Betsy Elliott of Elliott's Trans-Sierra Flight Service, David L. Trydahl and Kevin Ball of the White Mountain Research Station, Daniel Waterhead McCollum, Don Porcella, Greg, Madhu, and Sarina Porcella, Ethan, Iris and Walden Putterman, Mike Schillaci, Dan 'I'm freezing my ass off' Rothenburg, Dennis Junt, John Fisher, Steve Roper, Vittoria Lee Porcella, Royal Robbins, Peter Croft, Doug Robinson, Warren Harding, Eric Bjornstad, David Brower, Galen Rowell, Dave Wilson, R.J. Secor, Bill Oliver, Jules Eichorn, Glen Dawson, John Moynier, Claude Fiddler, Andy Stone, Luke Laeser, Jon Butler, Pete Lowry, Pete Dolan, Don Hampton, everyone at the Sierra Club Library, Ann Robertson, Mike, Penny, Jessica, Natalie and Kate Sandy, Dave Zendher, Kevin Sugar, Gary Powell, Bob and Sylvia Robertson, Michael Norgard, Jon Eck, Suresh Subramani, John Swanson, Dave Scheven, Ralph Judd, Don Craig, Dave Ingal, Suzanne, Tim, Nick, Vince, Eric, Mike, Mimi, and Elie Byrd and, of course, Gillian Burns.

INTRODUCTION

California's 14,000 foot peaks are a diverse and unique group of mountains. Thirteen of the Golden State's highest points are found in the Sierra Nevada. White Mountain is found in the White Mountain Range which lies to the east of the Sierra Nevada across the Owens Valley. Mount Shasta, considered part of the volcanic Cascades Range, is located in Northern California.

This guidebook is designed to supply information on the easiest route up each of California's 14,000 foot peaks. Unfortunately for the ambitious scrambler, there are several fourteeners in California whose ascent requires a basic knowledge of rock climbing. These peaks include, North Palisade, Starlight Peak, Thunderbolt Peak, Middle Palisade, and Polemonium Peak. Among the remaining fourteeners, Mount Williamson, Split Mountain, Mount Sill, Mount Shasta, Mount Russell, Mount Muir, and Mount Tyndall contain some steep sections on their routes. Mount Langley, White Mountain, and Mount Whitney, have walk-up routes on them and require little or no rock climbing preparation before an ascent. In the cases of Mount Whitney and Mount Sill, we have provided information on two routes on each peak with the intention of allowing you a choice regarding which route may be most suitable for your abilities.

Also, we have tried to provide you with accurate and up to date information on the conditions of these routes. We've also taken the time to enclose the latest information on Wilderness Permit requirements and a general listing of equipment that may be considered necessary for these routes.

State of the art guidelines for dealing with the number one problem in the backcountry of the Sierra Nevada, human waste and garbage, are included.

There are several other things in this book of value to someone attempting these peaks for the first time. A glossary of mountain geographical terms, a discussion of climbing safety, suggested descent routes, and what to do in case of emergency.

Be safe, keep the mountains clean, and good climbing!

Cam Burns and Steve Porcella

1 *Safety*

In the world of mountaineering, the mountaineer's single most important consideration is safety. The life of a climber, yours and your companion's, should always be your number one priority. Every aspect of your climb should revolve around safety, for amongst California's fourteen thousand foot peaks there is no room for error. Climbers young and old, experienced and inexperienced, have died on many of these high peaks. No route, no climb, no mountain, is worth the life of a human being.

Modern equipment, from good footwear to specific rock and ice climbing equipment, allows almost anyone with ambition the means with which to climb difficult routes. However, in addition to proper equipment and athletic ability, common sense and experience are necessary for safe and enjoyable climbs. Knowing when to back down off of a route is often the most important attribute one can have in the mountains. Knowing when to stop can often mean the difference between returning to a warm sleeping bag or spending, at the very least, a hypothermic night on a peak. If you find yourself trying to decide whether you should continue climbing or retreat, just remember that it is better to stay on the conservative side. The mountain will always be there for another day when the weather might be more favorable, or when your abilities and experience have improved.

Rope Handling

On some of the fourteeners in the Sierra Nevada, the easiest route can be quite difficult due to steepness, exposure, or the presence of ice. For these reasons we suggest the use of a rope for the ascent and descent of some of these peaks. The first step towards the use of a rope in safeguarding an ascent is to know proper rope handling techniques. There are many books on this subject, but unfortunately, books cannot substitute for actually getting out and practicing these techniques. Currently, there are many qualified guide schools that teach courses on rope handling technique. Unless you are proficient and experienced on Class 4 and 5 rock, we strongly suggest that that you take a course on rope handling technique before attempting some of the more difficult peaks. Check with your local mountaineering shop or outdoor club for listings of mountaineering and climbing schools and the courses that are available.

Your Ability

Once you know proper rope techniques such as belaying, anchoring, protection placement, and rappelling, the next step is to know your own limits and most importantly those of the people in your party. This goes back to our earlier point about knowing when to back down. There have been numerous incidents concerning climbers on the fourteeners where an experienced climber refused to acknowledge slower and less experienced climbers in the group. In almost every incidence someone was hurt or killed.

It is important to understand that your limit and judgement may be impaired by altitude, weather conditions, and rock conditions. Once again, common sense and conservative decisions are the key to safety and success.

Hypothermia and Altitude Sickness

These two ailments are probably indirectly responsible for more accidents in the mountains than anything else. Altitude sickness affects people differently and can sometimes affect a person at an elevation as low as 8,000 feet. Hypothermia can occur almost anywhere under any condition. There is not enough space in this guide book to go into a discussion of what hypothermia and altitude sickness are and their treatments. Therefore, it is your responsibility to know how altitude sickness and hypothermia can occur, and how they should be treated. Do not go into the mountains without this crucial information. Odds are that if you climb all of California's fourteeners, you will experience one or both of these conditions at some point. Written material on these two very important topics can be found at your local mountain shop or library.

Clothing

As far as clothing goes, we strongly argue against the use of cotton of any type except in the form of one T-shirt for extremely hot weather.   Obviously a good layering system involving polypropylene and or wool is essential, especially at high altitude. We recommend medium weight polypropylene long underwear, a double or triple layer of socks (no cotton!), sturdy boots or shoes, a pullover (wool or polyester type), and a light but waterproof jacket. A hat and pair of gloves aren't essential, but they can become very important if the weather turns cold or wet.

If you're planning to camp or bivouac in the mountains, a good sleeping bag can mean the difference between agony and ecstasy. Consult with your local mountain shop about what temperature bags would best be suited to the season and location of your climb. We have found 0° bags to be the minimum for 'under the stars' comfort during the summer. Both down-filled and poly-fiber-filled bags work well on California's fourteeners.

Rock/Icefall

On many of the routes in this guidebook, rock and icefall are minimal to non-existent. But, they are not completely unlikely. There is no way to prevent danger from ice and rockfall other than to avoid areas where it is frequent. In general, a couloir containing darkly stained snow or ice is usually indicative of present rock or ice fall. It is best to avoid the area even if it is, for example, the U-notch on North Palisade.

Rescue

When you plan a trip into the backcountry you should realize that you are on your own. Although there is a search and rescue available, you should plan as though it is not. Due to the ruggedness and isolation of the Sierra Nevada, it takes a great deal of time to reach and evacuate people with serious injuries. A seriously injured person can die of exposure due to the time required for rescue. So remember, it is especially important to take all necessary precautions to prevent an accident in the back-country. For the Sierra Nevada, Mount Shasta, and White Mountain, in the event of an accident or injury where a rescue is needed, the first thing to do is get to a phone and dial 911. For the Sierra Nevada and White Mountain, two other phone numbers which also work are:

Sheriff's Office in Lone Pine
(619) 876-5606

24 hour dispatch line
Sheriff's office in Independence
(619) 878 2441

To initiate a search, the party must be missing for a minimum of 24 hours and a member of the immediate family (next of kin) must request a search. Rescues are coordinated by the Sheriff's office which determines the involvement of other agencies such as the China Lake Mountain Rescue Group.

For Mount Shasta rescues, the Siskiyou County Sheriff's Department is responsible. They can be reached by dialing 911 or (916) 926-2552.

Weather

Check the weather reports before you leave. If there's a storm headed toward your proposed climbing goal, then perhaps you should reschedule your trip. Electrical storms are very common on all of California's high peaks, and people have been struck by lightning on them. If you see a few dark clouds appearing early in the morning, it might be wise to wait and see what happens, or even reschedule your climb for another day.   Be aware that storms can develop and be upon you within minutes especially on White Mountain or Shasta.

Bears

Bears are a real problem at Whitney Portal and Anvil Camp and are starting to populate Cottonwood Lakes Basin as well. They have not been seen in the North Fork of Lone Pine Creek, yet. In order to keep them from being attracted to new areas we suggest you tie up your food whenever possible and do not leave any items (dishes, wrappers, etc...) out that contain food remnants or odors.

CAUTION: This book is not intended to instruct the reader in the techniques of modern rock climbing or mountaineering. Both activities are hazardous, and it is the responsibility of the individual to learn and understand the proper techniques for safe participation in those activities. The individual also assumes all risks, damages, or injury which may result from improper use of this guidebook. Although we have given some information about rock climbing techniques, this guide is not meant as a substitute for personal instruction by a qualified person. Route descriptions detail the easiest line up the mountain. Many variations exist and it is up to the individual climbing party to make the best choices for their own safety.

2 *Wilderness Permits*

Regulations, quotas, and permit requirements can change over time. Therefore, we suggest that you CALL THE RANGER STATION OF THE AREA YOU ARE INTERESTED IN FOR CURRENT INFORMATION BEFORE YOU BEGIN YOUR TRIP. The following is the most up to date information available as of this writing:

MOUNT SHASTA

Wilderness permits are required for Mount Shasta. Currently there is no charge or quota for these permits. Overnight permits may be obtained at:

Mt. Shasta Ranger Station
204 West Alma Street
Mt. Shasta City, CA. 96067
Hours: 8:00 to 4:30 M-F
(916) 926-4511

Day use permits may be obtained at the Mt. Shasta Ranger Station during normal working hours, after hours, or at the Bunny Flat Trailhead. Overnight wilderness permits cannot be obtained at the Bunny Flat Trailhead. We suggest that you call the Mt. Shasta Ranger Station before you arrive in the town of Mount Shasta in order to receive the most current information available on wilderness permits.

WHITE MOUNTAIN

As of this writing, no wilderness permits are required for hiking to the summit of White Mountain, nor is any registration process in effect.

SIERRA NEVADA

Simply put, wilderness permits for overnight camping are required year round for hiking or climbing on all of the fourteen thousand foot peaks in the Sierra Nevada. A ranger can issue a citation if you are not carrying your permit. Permits are generally not required for day use (non-overnight trips). However, a day hike permit for Mt. Whitney is in the process of implementation and may be required at the publication date of this second edition.

During the heavy use period of the summer, all of the access trails are subject to quotas except for Red Lake Trail. Quotas limit the number of people allowed to camp overnight in the wilderness area each day. This helps to protect the wilderness resource and to provide a quality backcountry experience for everyone. For all trails, except the Mt. Whitney Trail and the North Fork of Lone Pine Creek Trail, the quota time period extends from the last Friday in June through September 15. For the Mt. Whitney Trail and the North Fork of Lone Pine Creek Trail the quota season is from May 22 to October 15. Normally one-half of the daily quota is available for advanced reservation, and the other half (along with any spaces not previously reserved) is available as first-come first-serve permits for that day. However, for the Mt. Whitney Trail all permits are available for prior registration. Cancelled or non-reserved permits are made available as first-come first-serve permits.

Trail quotas range from 6 per day for Georges Creek to 60 per day for the Cottonwood Lakes Trail. Outside the quota period, self issue permits are available at all Inyo National Forest Ranger Stations and some entrance stations.

FIRST-COME FIRST-SERVE PERMITS

Permits may be obtained on a first-come first-serve basis on the date of entry at certain locations and ranger stations. Trailheads, permit issuing stations, and hours are listed below.

Permits for **Bishop Pass via South Lake** are issued at:
Bishop Creek Entrance Station
Hours are 7:00 am to 3:30 pm, seven days a week,
from the last Friday in June through Sept. 15.
(619) 873-2527

This station is occupied by a ranger and is located about 9 miles west of Bishop on Highway 168. It is a kiosk on the right or north side of the road. The station is open each morning.

Permits for the **North Fork of Big Pine Creek Trail** and the **South Fork of Big Pine Creek Trail** out of Glacier Lodge are issued at:

Upper Sage Flat Campground
Hours are 7:00 to 7:30 am and 11:00 to 11:30 am,
from the last Friday in June through Sept. 15.

Upper Sage Flat Campground is about 8 miles west of Big Pine on Crocker Street near Glacier Lodge. Permits are issued by the campground host.

Permits for the **Red Lake Trail** can be issued at the Upper Sage Flat Campground because it is a non-quota trail or at:

White Mountain Ranger Station
798 North Main St.
Bishop, CA. 93514
(619) 873-2500
Hours are 7:00 am - 5:00 pm, Monday - Saturday, and
7:00 am - 3:00 pm, Sunday,
from the last Friday in June through Sept. 15.
Hours are 8:00 am - 4:30 pm, five days a week,
for the rest of the year.

Permits for **Shepherd Pass, Georges Creek, Cottonwood Lakes, North Fork of Lone Pine Creek** and the **Mt. Whitney Trail** are issued at: Mt. Whitney Ranger Station
640 South Main Street
Lone Pine, CA. 93545
(619) 876-6200
Hours are 7:00 am - 4:30 pm, seven days a week,
from the last Friday in June to Sept. 15.
Hours are 8:00 am - 4:30 pm, seven days a week,
May 22 to the last Friday in June and from Sept. 16 to Oct. 15.
Hours are 8:00 am - 4:30 pm, five days a week,
for the rest of the year.

Availability of first-come first-serve permits for the Mt. Whitney Trail are based on: 1) the number of cancellations for reserved permits for that day, and 2) the number of non-reserved permits remaining for that day.

Generally, first-come first-serve permits for the Mt. Whitney Trail range from rare to sometimes available on Mondays, Tuesdays or Wednesdays. Either way it is always a gamble getting first-come first-serve permits for this trail.

RESERVED PERMITS

The reservation system will be changing throughout the Sierra Nevada by 1996-unfortunately after the re-printing of this guide book. Therefore, the following information is based upon previous guidelines and may or may not be in effect currently.

First-come first-serve permits add an uncertainty with which many people feel uncomfortable, especially if their vacation time cannot be rescheduled. WE STRONGLY SUGGEST RESERVING YOUR PERMIT IN ADVANCE BY MAIL, rather than taking your chances of getting a permit on the day of your hike. Once again, we emphasize, call ahead first to the ranger station of the area you are interested in to get current and updated information.

Your envelope must be POSTMARKED BETWEEN MARCH 1 AND MAY 31 to obtain a wilderness permit for the upcoming summer quota period. Envelopes POSTMARKED BEFORE OR AFTER THIS TIME PERIOD WILL NOT BE PROCESSED if requesting summer quota period dates. When applying for a permit, make sure you mail the application to the correct ranger station and include the following :

1) $3.00 processing fee for each person in your group. For example, a party of four people must enclose $12.00 with their application. The check or money order should be made out to: "USDA Forest Service".

2) A printed or typed application (available from the district offices) or send detailed information regarding entry and exit dates, location of your camps, number of people in your party, and the address and phone number of someone to contact in case of emergency.

3) A list of at least two alternate dates in order of preference. Chances of gaining a permit are greater if the party size is kept small and starting dates are other than Friday, Saturday or holiday weekends.

For the **Bishop Pass Trail**, the **North Fork of Big Pine Creek Trail**, and the **South Fork of Big Pine Creek Trail**, send your fee and application to:

White Mountain Ranger Station
798 North Main St.
Bishop, CA. 93514
(619) 873-2500

The **Red Lake Trail** is a non-quota trail and therefore does not have a reservation period. Permits for the Red Lake Trail are obtained at any ranger or entrance station.

For **Shepherd Pass, Georges Creek, the North Fork of Lone Pine Creek Trail, the Mt. Whitney Trail**, and the **Cottonwood Lakes Trail**, mail your permit application to:

Mt. Whitney Ranger Station
Post Office Box 8
Lone Pine, CA 93545
(619) 876-6200

Permit guidelines for the Mt. Whitney Trail's summer quota period will be changing in 1996. Current guidelines are as follows.

ALL PERMITS for the Mt. Whitney Trail's summer quota period (May 22nd thru Oct 15) must be reserved between March 1 and May 31. In the first week of March the Mt. Whitney Ranger Station receives approximately 1,500 applications post-marked March 1. Almost all dates in July, August, and most weekends in September are completely booked by these applications. Therefore, we advise sending in your application **on March 1** and, as mentioned earlier, listing alternative dates you would like to hike the Mt. Whitney Trail.

Permits reserved in advance must be picked up in person at the location listed on the confirmation letter. Unless prior arrangements are made, any permit not picked up by 8:00 am is cancelled and made available to others on a first-come first-serve basis. Reserved permits may be picked up 24 hours in advance. These reserved permits are placed in an outside pick-up box next to the Ranger Station for your convenience. Entry into the wilderness is allowed only on the date stated on the permit.

3 Climbing and Wilderness Ethics

The preservation of the natural mountain environment, for the experience and enjoyment of future generations, is the responsibility of all who visit the high places.

THE ACCUMULATION OF HUMAN FECES AND TRASH IS THE SINGLE GREATEST PROBLEM IN THE SIERRA NEVADA TODAY.

For human feces a simple outline is as follows.

If you are in the Mount Whitney basin use the composting toilets. If you are off the trail in a large forest bury it deep (6 inches). If you are above timberline in a popular area pack it out. If you are above timberline and far, far away from people, spread it out as thinly as possible on a rock facing the sun. If you are on a glacier (ex; Palisade Glacier), use a crevasse. If you have to use toilet paper, always pack it out.

Those who carry out their feces from the popular routes are great mountaineers in the truest sense of style and deserve all the good karma they get. Small paper lunch bags (to poop in) filled with some lime or kitty litter and a strong, polyvinyl plastic bag (to store and carry the paper bags out), works wonders.

Other guidelines to keep the mountains pristine;

1). Carry out more trash than you carry in. Even if it is not yours.
2). Never camp or leave human feces, urine, toothpaste or soap within 100 feet of a water source.
3). Leave the area as you found it. Take apart fire rings you have created, put back rocks you have moved, and fill in tent ditches.
4). Don't place bolts on established routes or summits.
5). Don't make ducks or cairns. These can mislead people.
6). Use neutral colored rappel slings. Bright colors are unsightly.

4 *Climbing Grades*

CLASS 1- Hiking. Almost any footgear would be appropriate, from tennis shoes to mountain boots. (White Mountain Peak via the South Face, Mount Whitney via the Mt. Whitney Trail.)

CLASS 2- Hiking over rough terrain, where the hands may be used for balance. Hiking over boulders on a talus slope is a good example of Class 2 terrain. (Split Mountain via the North Ridge.)

CLASS 3- Steep rock or talus where handholds and footholds are used. A rope should be available for climbers not secure on steep or exposed terrain. Knowledge of belays is essential. A fall can cause moderate to serious injury. (East Face of Middle Palisade, Mountaineer's Route on Mt. Whitney.)

CLASS 4- Very steep, often vertical terrain usually involving great exposure. A rope should be used for safety. Knowledge of belays, anchors, and rappels is a prerequisite for a Class 4 route. A fall could be fatal. (Polemonium Peak, and Northwest Chute on Starlight Peak.)

CLASS 5- High angle rock climbing. Strenuous and sometimes difficult rock climbing moves required. A rope is essential. Nuts and friends are required for the safe upward progress of the leader in case he or she should fall. Rock climbing shoes are recommended. Class 5 is subdivided into fourteen categories of increasing difficulty (5.0 to 5.14). (Summit Pinnacle on Starlight Peak, Summit Monolith on Thunderbolt Peak.)

5 Getting to the Mountains

Nearly all of California's 14,000 foot peaks are located within a one hundred mile radius of the town of Bishop, California. Bishop lies directly east of San Jose, and directly north of Los Angeles on the eastern side of the Sierra Nevada. It can be reached by Highway 395 from the north or south. The other towns mentioned in this guidebook, Big Pine, Independence, and Lone Pine, lie south of Bishop 15, 40, and 58 miles respectively. Route descriptions for the fourteen thousand foot peaks of the Sierra Nevada begin at these towns.

To get to Bishop from the north (San Francisco, Merced, Sacramento) it is best to drive east towards Yosemite and get on Highway 120. After crossing Tioga pass, turn south (right) onto Highway 395. Tioga Pass is subject to winter closure and may not open until late spring.

From the south (Los Angeles and San Diego) the quickest way to get to Bishop is via I-5 north to Highway 14 north. Continue on 14 until it merges with Highway 395 near Inyokern. You will pass through Lone Pine, Independence, and Big Pine on the way up Highway 395 to Bishop.

White Mountain Peak is reached by driving east from the town of Big Pine on Highway 168. The description for White Mountain Peak in this guidebook begins at Big Pine.

Mount Shasta lies in the northern portion of the state and is best reached by driving north on I-5 from most cities in California. The route description for getting to the base of the peak begins at the town of Mount Shasta which is 59 miles north of Redding, California on I-5.

Map 1 — The general location of the fifteen fourteen thousand foot peaks in California.

6 *Mount Langley* *14,027 feet*

Mount Langley, the southernmost 14,000 foot peak in the Sierra Nevada, has more in common with California's desert mountains than with its high Sierra relatives to the north. The mountain's summit is covered with a dry layer of white granitic gravel and vegetation is almost non-existent. Indians were more than likely the first on the summit, but William Bellows made the first recorded ascent of Mount Langley in 1864.

CLIMBING MOUNT LANGLEY

Cottonwood Lakes Approach:

The easiest, safest, and most popular way to achieve Mount Langley's summit is via Cottonwood Lakes and Old Army Pass which can be done in one very long day from the Cottonwood Lakes Trailhead. Although the round trip is about twenty-one miles, the amount of elevation gain from Cottonwood Lakes to the summit is only 4,000 feet. A more leisurely ascent can be made with a camp at Cottonwood Lakes, which are halfway to the peak.

The odometer chart and Map 2 describe the drive to the Cottonwood Lakes Trailhead from the town of Lone Pine.

Odometer Reading	Route Description at the Odometer Reading
0 mi.	Corner of Hwy 395 and Whitney Portal Road in Lone Pine. Go west on Whitney Portal Road.
3.1 mi.	Turn left (south) on Horseshoe Meadows Road.

21.3 mi.   A sign reads "Trail Pass, Cottonwood Pass (arrow forward), New Army Pass, Cottonwood Lakes (arrow right)". Turn right (north). (Note: It is important that you turn right here. If you continue straight you will reach the "Cottonwood Pass Trailhead", which is not the correct trailhead. Many hikers have lost hours trying to correct this mistake.)

21.9 mi.   Arrive at Cottonwood Lakes Trailhead parking lot. The trailhead is marked by a signed interpretive display.

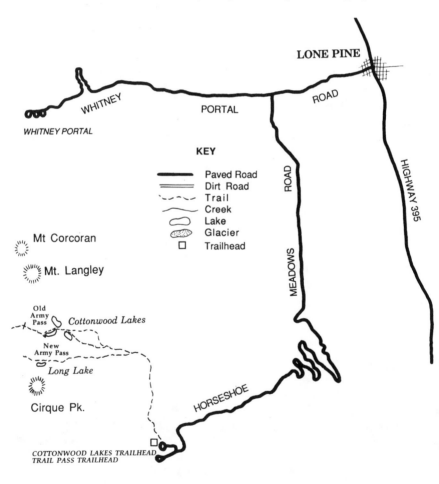

Map 2 — Mount Langley

1) Cottonwood Lakes Trail to Army Pass. Class 1-2.

The Cottonwood Lakes Trail leaves the Trailhead parking area at its northwest end. Follow it all the way to the Cottonwood Lakes. From the first lake, Mount Langley will become obvious. It is the large peak to the north. Although the summit is not visible at this point, the expansive granite cliff of the south face is in plain view. The summit is just beyond the mountain's visible high point.

From Cottonwood Lakes, the next objective becomes Old Army Pass to the west. It is very important that you do not confuse Old Army Pass with New Army Pass. New Army Pass is reached by taking a trail to Long Lake and High Lake. Old Army Pass is directly west of the three large lakes in the Cottonwood Lakes basin and is a rough and unmaintained trail. If you are not already on a trail (there are many in this basin) that leads to Old Army Pass, hike cross-country towards the large southwestern Cottonwood Lake. Once at the lake, follow its northern shoreline and you should pick up a trail that will lead you up and over the pass.

After the pass has been gained, the remainder of the climb is a fairly straightforward march up steep gravel to the north. Continue hiking until the summit plateau is reached, then head east, to the summit itself. The best way to know when to head east is when the

Old Army Pass. The trail goes around the right side of the lake and switchbacks up to the top of the pass.

Shot at 15,000 feet, this photograph shows the summit and the final portion of the west slope of Mount Langley (Route 1).

dramatic north face is reached; it will drop out from under your feet. At this point head east.

<u>Descent</u>: The easiest descent of Mount Langley is made by returning down the Cottonwood Lakes Trail via Old Army Pass (Route 1).

7 *Mount Muir 14,015 feet*

From the west, Mount Muir is a fairly inconspicuous bump on a very high ridge. From the east, however, Mount Muir appears to stand as a separate mountain in its own right. It is not known who made the first ascent of Muir but it was probably done from the west, in the vicinity of the Mt. Whitney Trail.

CLIMBING MOUNT MUIR

The quickest and easiest way to climb Mount Muir is via the Mt. Whitney Trail that passes within a few feet of Mount Muir's summit on the way to Mount Whitney. In fact, if you plan to climb Mount Whitney, the short detour to Mount Muir's summit will only add an hour or so to your climb.

2) Mount Muir via the Mt. Whitney Trail. Class 3.

Reaching the base of Mount Muir is one of the more straightforward approach hikes in the Sierra Nevada. Use the mileage chart and Map 3 in the Mount Whitney Chapter (p. 23-24) for directions to the Whitney Portal from the town of Lone Pine.

After parking at the Whitney Portal, follow the Mt. Whitney Trail for approximately 6 miles. After 6 miles, an extensive bivouac area called Trail Camp is reached. There are many campsites located here including a toilet facility.

From the Trail Camp area, Mount Muir lies directly west and should be obvious. It is the high point lying just north of the point

The east face of Mount Muir.
The Mt. Whitney Trail is out of the photo to the left.

where the Mt. Whitney Trail crosses the Sierra Crest.

To reach the western slope of Mount Muir, simply continue up the Mt. Whitney Trail. The trail steepens and goes through a series of switchbacks before it gains a low point in the crest of the ridge. This low point is known as Trail Crest Pass. Two-tenths of a mile past Trail Crest Pass, the Mt. Whitney Trail will intersect with the John Muir Trail. Continue approximately 500 yards beyond the intersection. At this point you should look to the east and decide where you want to begin climbing towards Mount Muir. The terrain to the summit of Muir is a moderately steep boulder field, and is basically the same anywhere from the west. The final portion to the summit is composed of a short section of Class 3 rock with many variations.

<u>Descent</u>: The easiest descent is to down-climb your ascent route and follow the Mt. Whitney Trail out.

Mount Muir from the Mt. Whitney Trail.

8 *Mount Whitney 14,495 feet*

The top of Mount Whitney is the single most sought after 14,000 foot summit in North America. Thousands of hikers, climbers, and curious trekkers of all ages achieve Whitney's lofty summit every year. On a warm summer day, it is not uncommon to see more than 200 people enjoying the magnificent view from the highest point in the contiguous United States.

Whitney was first climbed by three fishermen, Charles Begole, Albert Johnson, and John Lucas on September 17, 1873.

CLIMBING MOUNT WHITNEY

The quickest and easiest way to climb Mount Whitney is via the Mt. Whitney Trail from the Whitney Portal. The Mt. Whitney Trail is the most frequented trail throughout the Sierra Nevada. The trail sees so many people that toilets facilities have been built at Outpost Camp and Trail Camp to keep human waste out of the already polluted lakes and streams.

Whitney Portal Approach:
The following odometer chart and Map 3 (p. 24) describe the drive to the Whitney Portal from the town of Lone Pine:

Odometer Reading	Route Description at the Odometer Reading
0 mi.	Start at the corner of Hwy 395 and Whitney Portal Road in Lone Pine. Go west on Whitney Portal Road.
13 mi.	Whitney Portal.

The parking lot at the end of the road is often full and it is sometimes necessary to park in designated overflow parking lots. The trailhead is marked by a kiosk and is near the end of the road on the north (right) side of the canyon.

3) Mt. Whitney Trail. Class 1.

Winding slowly up through pine trees, small lakes, and spectacular vistas, the Mt. Whitney Trail eventually gains over 6,000 feet in elevation from the Whitney Portal. The Mt. Whitney Trail is the easiest and safest route up Mount Whitney.

The trail starts at an elevation of 8,400 feet and crosses three streams before it reaches Lone Pine Lake, 2.5 miles from the Portal. Another mile up the trail is Outpost Camp (elevation 10,350 ft.) which is a good place to camp early on the trail. Farther up the trail at 6 to 6.5 miles from the trailhead is Trail Camp (elevation 12,040 ft.). This is the best place to camp in preparation for an attempt on

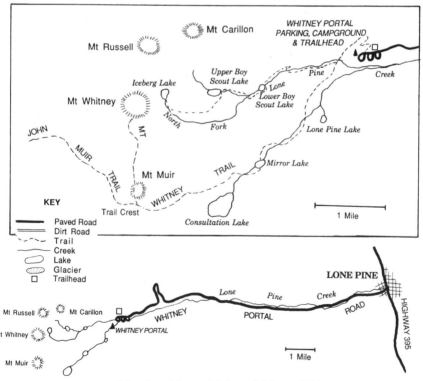

Map 3 — Mount Muir and Mount Whitney

the summit of Mt. Whitney. It is about 5 miles farther to the summit so an early start is advised.

The most obvious obstacle after leaving Trail Camp is the seemingly endless series of switchbacks to reach Trail Crest. 99 switchbacks have been counted for this section of the hike. During early summer or late spring, caution on the trail is advised because of lingering ice and steep snow on portions of the upper switchbacks. The Mount Whitney Ranger District Office in Lone Pine can inform you on the conditions of the trail and if an ice axe is recommended.

After Trail Crest (elevation 13,800 ft.) the trail enters Sequoia National Park just south of Mount Muir and traverses the Whitney Massif on the west side of Muir, Third Needle, Day and Keeler Needles. The trail twists and turns amongst the fractured granite blocks gradually gaining in elevation to reach the summit of Mt. Whitney. The entire ascent from Whitney Portal requires nothing more than stamina, determination, some acclimatization, and a good pair of hiking boots. It is almost impossible to lose this trail.

East Face Approach via North Fork of Lone Pine Creek Trail. Class 2-3:

The standard approach for the east face of Mt. Whitney and Mt. Russell starts on the Mt. Whitney Trail. After one mile it follows the North Fork of Lone Pine Creek. This gorge is narrow, brush-filled and extremely steep. With a pack it will be the most challenging part of getting to the peaks. The Forest Service strongly recommends that anyone who uses this approach or camps at the east face of Mt. Whitney packs out all human feces.

The key to starting up the North Fork of Lone Pine Creek Trail is selecting the correct creek to follow. The North Fork of Lone Pine Creek is almost one mile from the Mt. Whitney Trailhead and is the second creek to be crossed on the Mt. Whitney Trail. Cross the creek and stay on the south (left) side. The trail is steep, not maintained, and hard to follow, but it still is the best way to ascend the North Fork of Lone Pine Creek.

The first section of the trail winds up through trees next to the creek and crosses a long section of large boulders below a north facing wall. Eventually, granite slabs on the left pinch the canyon closed. Above this point the canyon is choked with alder and is very difficult to negotiate. The key here is to head north across the creek towards the granite wall on the other side of the creek. Once near the wall, scramble through alder towards a large foxtail pine tree on a ledge. This foxtail pine can be seen before you cross the creek and is shown in the photo below. Once you have reached the tree, a series of ledges lead east for approximately 100 yards. This ledge system is known locally as Clyde's Traverse (also known as Ebersbacher Ledges), and they allow one to get high above the life-choking alder of the canyon.

Once you have completed Clyde's Traverse, the dense alder in the gorge can become a memory. The ledges end above the most difficult part of the gorge and the hike resumes as an easy, somewhat faint trail up to Lower Boy Scout Lake. Lower Boy Scout Lake (elevation 10,320) is a small lake in transition to a meadow. At the east end of Lower Boy Scout Lake, cross the stream using the obvious boulders and logs. From here, the trail wanders through tall pines around the south (left) side of Lower Boy Scout Lake. Several variations of the trail will soon merge together as you ascend the steep boulder field to the south of the tumbling stream. After gaining the top of this steep slope it is best to cross to the north side of the drainage, over sloping wet granite slabs, before continuing west towards Upper Boy Scout Lake. Caution is advised while crossing these slabs because slippery lichen abounds. Above the slabs the Southeast Slopes To East Arete on Mount Russell (Route 5) diverges from the North Fork of Lone Pine Creek. The southeast facing gravel and talus slope on the right or north side of

Route through Clyde's Traverse (Ebersbacher Ledges).
Arrow points to the foxtail pine mentioned in the text.

The North Fork Trail from Lower Boy Scout Lake.

the drainage is the starting point for the hike up Mount Russell.

To reach the east face of Mount Whitney and the start of the Mountaineer's Route, turn southwest when you reach the east end of Upper Boy Scout Lake (elevation 11,300 ft.). Climb up talus using a faint trail towards an obvious low point in the ridge. From this point, after hiking west for a short distance, the incredible eastern faces of Day Needle, Keeler Needle and Mount Whitney should be obvious. Continue west directly towards these peaks. After a mile and half of moraine hiking, a faint trail will turn north (right) up steep gravel towards a low point in the ridge that you have been hiking around since leaving Upper Boy Scout Lake. Ascend this last steep section of steep gravel and rock and you will arrive at Iceberg Lake (elevation 12,240 feet). This is the best place to bivouac for climbing the Mountaineer's Route on Mount Whitney.

4) Mountaineer's Route. Class 3.

Photo taken from the Iceberg Lake Basin showing the east face of Mt. Whitney and the Mountaineer's Route to the notch.

     This route was first climbed by John Muir, solo, on October 21, 1873. This large gully provides the easiest method of ascending the eastern side of Mount Whitney. It gains the obvious notch just north (right, when viewed from below the east face) of the summit. The gully is often snow-filled and has many loose rocks in the form of gravel and talus. Enter the northern portion of the gully and ascend steep snow and gravel to the notch.

Once the notch has been gained, the Mountaineer's Route continues directly west, traversing several chutes on the north slope of the mountain. It is important to hike west from the notch for about 300 yards before an easy hike to the west sloping summit plateau becomes evident. The summit, which lies back to the east, is obvious from this point.

The only equipment absolutely necessary for this route is a good pair of boots. An ice-axe is thoroughly recommended if it is early in the year and snow is prevalent in the gully. If you are inexperienced on moderately steep snow, a small pair of instep crampons or their equivalent can be comforting. It is important to note that small sections of this route are choked with ice all year long.

<u>Descent</u>: The easiest descent is the Mt. Whitney Trail (Route 3) which returns to the Whitney Portal. However, if you've climbed the Mountaineer's Route and are camped near Iceberg Lake, your best bet is to descend that route. Following the Mt. Whitney Trail down will put you miles from the base of the east face of Whitney.

Climber traversing the north facing slope towards the notch of the Mountaineer's Route after summiting Whitney.

9 *Mount Russell 14,086 feet*

Mount Russell is an elegant mountain. Glacial ice could never have created a more perfectly sculptured peak. Sweeping chasms and smooth twisting ridges abut the southern side of the mountain like the flying buttresses of a mediaeval church. The summit itself is like a knife-edged gable, with steep walls falling away on all sides. There are two summits over 14,000 feet on Mount Russell, with the higher of the two being the western summit.

Mount Russell was not climbed until relatively late compared to the other fourteeners. Norman Clyde made the first ascent, solo, on June 24, 1926.

CLIMBING MOUNT RUSSELL

5) Southeast Slopes To East Arete. Class 3.

This is the original route used by Norman Clyde on the first ascent. It is also one of the easiest routes, not to mention the most popular, on the mountain. The first objective in climbing the East Arete is to reach the saddle between Mount Russell and Mount Carillon. This climb starts just below the eastern shore of Upper Boy Scout Lake and ascends a large gravel slope on the north side of the North Fork of Lone Pine Creek Canyon. A detailed description of how to get to Upper Boy Scout Lake is given in Chapter 8 under the headings "Whitney Portal Approach" (p. 23-24) and "East Face Approach via North Fork of Lone Pine Creek Trail" (p. 25-27) along with Map 3 (p. 24).

The southeast face of Mount Russell. Route 5 is shown beginning below the eastern shore of Upper Boy Scout Lake. The summit of Mount Russell is on the left.

From an area about 800 yards east of Upper Boy Scout Lake, climb the enormous gravel slope in a northwest direction. This slope ascends the southeastern section of Mount Russell for well over a mile and seems interminable. However, you will eventually reach the saddle near the eastern end of the East Arete. This long ridge proceeds west for nearly a mile, joining with the eastern summit. The eastern summit is joined to the western higher summit by a knife-blade ridge. Staying exactly on the ridge for its length is impossible, and there are numerous places where it is necessary to drop down on the northern side of the ridge.

Descent: The easiest way to descend Mount Russell is to use the same route you came up (The Southeast Slopes To East Arete - Route 5).

10 *Mount Williamson 14,375 feet*

Simply stated, Mount Williamson is an enormous peak. It is one of the tallest peaks in the nation, and in California, it is second in elevation only to Mount Whitney. From Highway 395, Mount Williamson can usually be seen from fifty miles away.

The first recorded ascent of Mount Williamson was performed by W.L. Hunter and C. Mulholland in 1884 via the rugged, trailless drainage known as Georges Creek Canyon.

CLIMBING MOUNT WILLIAMSON

As of this writing, there are areas around Mount Williamson and Mount Tyndall that are restricted to access during certain times of the year. It is wise to call the Mount Whitney Ranger District Office in Lone Pine before you begin a trip into the Williamson area. You must make sure the time that you have planned for your trip does not conflict with the access restrictions currently in place. We have listed the current access times but these may be subject to change in the future.

The Bighorn Zoological Preserve is open from December 15 to July 15. Shepherd Pass is open all year round. Because it is located within the preserve, Mount Williamson is only open to climbing from December 15 to July 15.

Shepherd Pass Trail Approach:

The following odometer chart and Map 4 (p. 34) explain how to get to the Shepherd Pass Trailhead:

Odometer Reading	Route Description at the Odometer Reading
0 mi.	Start at the corner of Highway 395 and Market Street in Independence. Go west (towards the Sierra Nevada) on Market Street. Outside town, Market Street becomes Onion Valley Road.
4.4 mi.	Turn left (south) on Foothill Road (dirt).
5.5 mi.	Road forks, follow the right (west) fork. Also, you'll see a sign reading "Shepherd Pass Trailhead".
7.4 mi.	Fork in road. Go right. There is a sign reading "Shepherd Pass Trailhead" here.
7.9 mi.	Fork in road. Go right.
8.6 mi.	Fork in road. Go right.
8.8 mi.	Symmes Creek (Shepherd Pass Trailhead). Parking. pH toilet present.

There is a large parking lot at the end of the road, with a kiosk and from here it is a long (about 10 miles) hike to Shepherd Pass. It is not uncommon to take two days from the car to make the hike to Shepherd Pass. From the trailhead, the Shepherd Pass Trail follows Symmes Creek for about a mile before it turns south (left) and switchbacks numerous times up to the top of Symmes Saddle. From this ridge, the north face of Mount Williamson can be seen to the south. The trail drops southwest and continues into Shepherd Creek Canyon.

There are several good campsites in this canyon. Mahogany Flat is the first camping area encountered on the Shepherd Pass Trail. The most popular camping area is a little farther along the trail and is called Anvil Camp (elevation 10,040 ft.). Many climbers make camp at Anvil Camp due to its protection from the wind. No campfires are allowed in Anvil Camp or Mahogany Flat. The hike from Anvil Camp to start the climb on Williamson is a long one and definitely requires an early start.

To get closer to Mt. Tyndall and Mt. Williamson, continue on the Shepherd Pass Trail to Shepherd Pass. In late summer, the pass is nothing more than a steep talus hike (Class 2). In early summer,

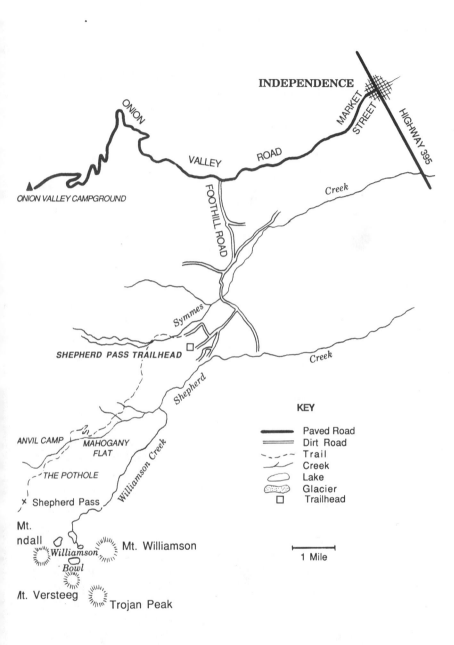

Map 4 — Mount Williamson and Mount Tyndall

an ice axe can be very useful when snow covers much of the pass. Once on top of Shepherd Pass, two options are available. If you are climbing Mt. Tyndall, it is best to hike southwest to the north side of the peak while looking for a place to camp. If you are going to climb Williamson, then hike southeast to a large basin known as the Williamson Bowl (elevation 12,200 ft.). A 300 foot drop over talus and boulders is the final obstacle to the first large lake in the Williamson Bowl. There are four large lakes in this basin and gravel bivy sites can usually be found near them. By camping in the bowl, you'll be able to climb both Williamson and Tyndall on consecutive days.

6) West Face. Class 3.

This route was first climbed by Joseph N. LeConte, R.H. Butler, E.B. Gould, T. Parker, G. Cosgrove, A. Elston, and A.G. Eells on July 10, 1903. This is the most popular route on the mountain and is fairly straight forward. We recommend this route and suggest that you take a rope and a few nuts, or be totally comfortable on Class 3 rock.

After entering the Williamson Bowl from the north, hike south towards the second lake in the bowl. You will pass the first lake on

Shepherd Creek Canyon with Shepherd Pass on the right and
Mount Williamson on the left.

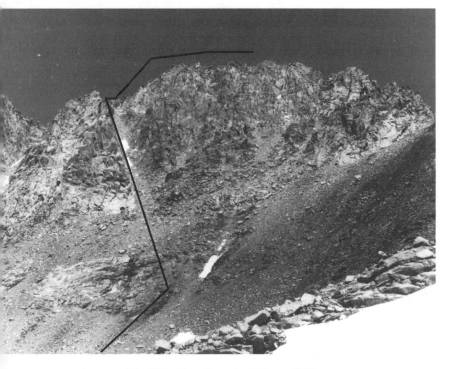

The West Face Route on Mount Williamson.

your right (west) that lies at the base of the impressive east face of Mount Tyndall. Directly east of the second lake lies the West Face Route on Mount Williamson.

On the southern portion of the west face of Mount Williamson is a prominent rock band along the base of the mountain. This rock band contains a number of black water marks. Climb towards the most prominent black water mark and ascend the talus just to the right (south) of it. Above the black water mark, enter and climb a large chute for about one thousand feet. At the top of the chute, a broken rocky cliff blocks further progress. A few feet to the left (northeast) is a small notch that looks out upon the north face of Mount Williamson and the Owens Valley. To continue to the summit, traverse right (southeast) below the rocky cliff for about twenty feet to a narrow cleft. Climb up this cleft, which is moderate Class 3 and one pitch long. The summit plateau is gained at the top of this pitch. From here it is a short walk to the South (main) Summit.

Climbers in the large chute of the West Face Route.

<u>Descent</u>: We suggest descending the West Face Route (Route 6) since it is the easiest. A careful down-climb or short rappel of the Class 3 section is required.

A rope can be very useful on the final Class 3 crux of the West Face Route.

11 *Mount Tyndall 14,018 feet*

An incredibly picturesque peak, Mount Tyndall's eastern escarpment falls away dramatically, giving it a shape that imitates many other peaks in the Sierra Nevada; Mount Whitney for one. Mount Tyndall was first climbed by Clarence King and Richard Cotter on July 6, 1864.

CLIMBING MOUNT TYNDALL

The quickest and easiest way to climb Mount Tyndall is via the Northwest Ridge (Route 7) after following the Shepherd Pass Trail from Owens Valley.

Refer to the Mount Williamson Chapter for a route description and map to the Shepherd Pass Trailhead as well as a trail description to Shepherd Pass (p. 32-35).

Approach via the Shepherd Pass Trailhead:

After gaining Shepherd Pass, the north sides of both Mount Williamson and Mount Tyndall come into view. Tyndall's sharp eastern escarpment is not visible, but can be seen by heading south, into the Williamson Bowl as described in the Williamson Chapter.

The most obvious ridge from Shepherd Pass is the northwest ridge which descends to a point about a half mile west (right, when viewed from Shepherd Pass) of the pass. Hike to the base of this ridge to reach Route 7. The surrounding area is fairly flat and appropriate for camping (elevation 12,010 ft.). However, you may have to hike further west to find water.

The north side of Mount Tyndall. The Northwest Ridge (Route 7) ascends the right side of the prominent rock rib.

7) Northwest Ridge. Class 2.

The first ascent of this route is unknown. From Shepherd Pass, The Northwest Ridge Route can be seen starting near the base of a prominent sloping ridge that descends from the summit northward to a point about a half mile west of Shepherd Pass. The route ascends the north sloping ridge while staying to the right or west side (west) of a rock rib. Near the top of the north facing slope, the rock rib on the left (east) joins up with a ridge that rises from the right (northwest). Where these two ridges meet is a notch. Hike through the notch, by-passing the rock tower on its right side (west). Stay to the right (west) while scrambling up the final summit ridge to the top of the peak. The sheer east face drops away to the left, and caution should be taken not to wander too close to the edge.

Descent: The quickest, easiest, and safest descent of Mount Tyndall is via the Northwest Ridge (Route 7).

12 *Split Mountain 14,058 feet*

The shape of Split Mountain is unique. A steep, polished gully divides the center of both the east face and the west face. Both of these gullies meet at the top of the mountain and are connected by a notch that splits the peak into twin summits.

The first recorded ascent of Split Mountain was made by Frank Saulque and four others by an unknown route in July, 1887.

CLIMBING SPLIT MOUNTAIN

The easiest and quickest way to climb Split Mountain is via the North Ridge (Route 8). This is the only route that ever receives traffic, and it is the only route that we recommend since all the other easy routes require several days of arduous cross-country travel to reach the appropriate mountain face.

East Face Approach:

The east face of Split Mountain and The North Ridge Route are best reached by hiking the Red Lake Trail to Red Lake. As of this writing, the road to the Red Lake Trailhead requires a vehicle with high clearance and four-wheel drive.

To reach the trailhead for the Red Lake Trail, please follow the accompanying odometer chart and Map 5 (p. 43) paying special attention to the descriptions.

Odometer Reading	Route Description at the Odometer Reading
0 mi.	Start at the corner of Hwy 395 and Crocker St. in Big Pine. Go west on Crocker St. towards Glacier Lodge.
2.5 mi.	Crocker St. (also known as Glacier Lodge Rd.) crosses Big Pine Creek. Take a dirt road that cuts left off Glacier Lodge Rd. heading south. The road quickly forks with one branch heading west, parallel to Glacier Lodge Rd., and the other southwest. Take the southwest (left) branch. This dirt road is in good condition.
2.6 mi.	Between 2.5 and 2.6 miles, three dirt roads are crossed. Continue straight.
6.4 mi.	Cross a cattle guard.
6.6 mi.	Cross a road that cuts off to the right.
8.2 mi.	Continue straight (south) through a four-way intersection.
8.7 mi.	Pass through a fence. A wire gate may be strung across the road. Be sure to close the gate after passing through.
9.4 mi.	Continue to the left passing a road that turns to the right. The road will now wind around, become rough, and cross two creek beds.
9.8 mi.	Continue to the left passing another road that turns to the right.
10.0 mi.	Pass through a gate and once again make sure to close the gate after yourself.
10.9 mi.	Continue straight past a road which turns sharply to the left.
11.3 mi.	Follow the road to Tinnemaha Creek which curves south at the intersection. While following this road, a range fence should be on your left.

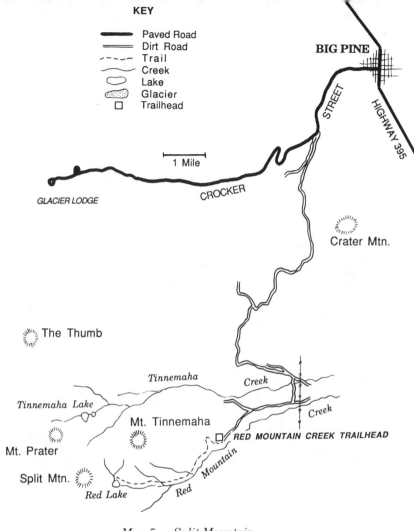

KEY

- ▬▬▬ Paved Road
- ══ Dirt Road
- - - - Trail
- ～ Creek
- ◯ Lake
- ⬭ Glacier
- ☐ Trailhead

BIG PINE

STREET

HIGHWAY 395

1 Mile

GLACIER LODGE

CROCKER

Crater Mtn.

The Thumb

Tinnemaha   *Creek*

Tinnemaha Lake

Creek

Mt. Tinnemaha

RED MOUNTAIN CREEK TRAILHEAD ☐

Mt. Prater

Split Mtn.

Red Lake

Red   Mountain

Map 5 — Split Mountain

11.8 mi. Turn right (heading west) on the road marked 10501A.

12.4 mi. Continue straight past a road that branches left.

12.6 mi. Continue straight again past a road that branches left.

12.9 mi. Take the left branch marked 10501 at the fork in the road. The road winds left then right and ends near a forest service kiosk. The actual trail starts 100 yards northwest of the kiosk at a small clump of trees.

The trail to Red Lake is steep, narrow, poorly marked, and often dust choked during summer months. Be sure to take water for the beginning of this hike. The trail follows along the right side of the canyon all the way to Red Lake. Red Mountain Creek usually has water, but it is a scramble to reach from the trail.

East face of Split Mountain. North Ridge (Route 8)
from Red Lake is shown.

8) North Ridge. Class 3.

First ascent Jules Eichorn and Norman Clyde, date unknown. Except for one section of loose Class 3 talus, it is almost entirely Class 1-2.

From Red Lake (elevation 10,460 ft.) hike northwest up the talus filled creek drainage that is the inlet to Red Lake. This drainage, composed of several minor benches, curves around the northeast corner of Split Mountain towards a low point or saddle in the ridge between Mt. Prater and Split Mountain. The last several hundred feet of climbing to the top of the saddle consists of Class 3 rubble and talus. Once on the saddle, follow the huge northern

From the saddle between Split Mountain and Mount Prater, the final hike up the north ridge of Split Mountain is an easy talus slope.

slope (Class 1) of the mountain up to the summit.

<u>Descent</u>: The easiest, safest, and fastest descent from the summit of Split Mountain is via your route of ascent, the North Ridge (Route 8).

13 *Middle Palisade 14,040 feet*

The east face of Middle Palisade towers over the South Fork Basin of Big Pine Creek. At the base of the peak's eastern face lies the Middle Palisade Glacier. On August 26, 1922, Francis Farquhar and Ansel F. Hall, Park Naturalist of Yosemite National Park, made the first ascent of Middle Palisade.

CLIMBING MIDDLE PALISADE

The East Face (Route 9), is the easiest route to the top of Middle Palisade. The following route description and Map 6 show how to get to the east face.

East Face Approach via South Fork of Big Pine Creek Trail:
The east face is best reached by parking near Glacier Lodge, and hiking the South Fork of Big Pine Creek Trail. The following is a mileage chart describing the route to Glacier Lodge:

Odometer Reading	Route Description at the Odometer Reading
0 mi.	Start at the corner of Highway 395 and Crocker Street in Big Pine. Go west on Crocker Street towards Glacier Lodge.
13.5 mi.	Turnoff to the right leads to the only overnight parking for backpackers.

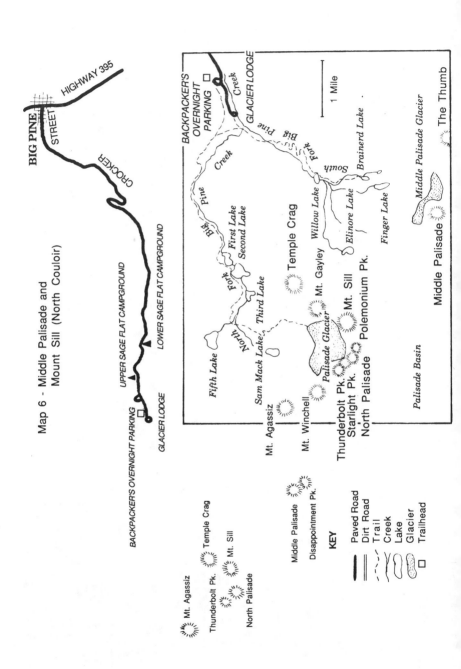

Map 6 - Middle Palisade and Mount Sill (North Couloir)

14.0 mi.   Glacier Lodge. Backpackers and climbers can be dropped off here to save some walking. The South Fork of Big Pine Creek Trail starts at the end of Crocker Street which is about a hundred yards to the north of Glacier Lodge.

Start hiking the trail from the end of Crocker Street. After about 1/4 of a mile, a sign designates the start of the South Fork of Big Pine Creek Trail. The trail heads south along the South Fork of Big Pine Creek. After about a mile of hiking, the trail will switchback up a prominent rock buttress to eventually top out near Willow Lake. During wet times of the year, Willow Lake is home to the breeding ground for billions of mosquitoes. If they are in season you might want to sprint through this area to avoid being eaten alive. The trail, which sometimes may be narrow or faint due to its infrequent use, continues in a southern direction to Brainerd Lake (elevation 10,240 ft.), a beautiful little lake with several nice campsites.

There are two possible ways to reach the east face of Middle Palisade from Brainerd Lake. One involves hiking west around the

The South Fork of Big Pine Creek Basin with the Thumb on the left and Middle Palisade on the right.

lake and gradually moving up ledges to Finger Lake. The other leads around the east side of Brainerd Lake, and follows the inlet creek to eventually by-pass two small lakes on the right (west). Beyond the second small lake, turn right (west), hiking beneath a large rock prow several hundred feet high. Several basins containing small glacial tarns are encountered. The east facing glaciers at the base of Middle Palisade and Disappointment Peak are soon reached.

East Face Route on Middle Palisade.

9) East Face. Class 3.

This is the easiest and most straightforward way to get to the summit of Middle Palisade. The first ascent party is unknown.
There are many variations to this route. The variations mainly involve crossing into alternate couloirs or following the aretes that

border the gullies. The following description chronicles the most popular route for gaining the summit of Middle Palisade.

The route begins on the right (north) portion of the Middle Palisade Glacier. Climb up the snow of the glacier between a rock moraine on the left (south) and the small rock ridge that separates the Middle Palisade Glacier from Clyde Glacier to the north. About halfway up the snow, climb onto a ledge/chimney system which leads up the buttress to the right. Follow the ledge into a large broad couloir and climb up this couloir. When the couloir begins to end, cross over to the next couloir to the north (right). After a short distance this couloir will divide. Both the right and left branches of the couloir are about the same difficulty. Both reach notches to the north and south of the summit respectively.

Much of this route is continuous Class 3 with some portions of Class 4 encountered if climbers get off-route. A rope is recommended if you are not totally comfortable on Class 3 rock. The first ledge/chimney system becomes somewhat exposed and can be the most difficult part of the climb.

Descent: The easiest route of descent is the East Face (Route 9).

14 *Mount Sill 14,162 feet*

As with so many mountains all over the world, the story of Mount Sill is linked to a taller neighbor, in this case, North Palisade. On July 24, 1903, James Hutchinson, J.K. Moffitt, Robert Pike, and Joseph N. LeConte made the first ascent after failing to get to the top of North Palisade.

CLIMBING MOUNT SILL

Mount Sill has two routes which differ in their approaches and difficulties. The quickest route to get to is the North Couloir (Route 10) on the north side of Mount Sill. The easiest route to climb is the Southwest Chutes (Route 11) on the west side of the peak. The two approaches used to get to these routes are the North Fork of Big Pine Creek Trail and the Bishop Pass Trail via South Lake, respectively.

North Face Approach via North Fork of Big Pine Creek Trail:
The north face of Mt. Sill, and the northeast faces of all the other 14,000 foot peaks of the Palisade region, are best reached by driving to Glacier Lodge. The following is a mileage chart describing the drive to Glacier Lodge (Refer to Map 6 on page 47):

Odometer Reading	Route Description at the Odometer Reading
0 mi.	Start at the corner of Highway 395 and Crocker Street in Big Pine. Go west on Crocker Street towards Glacier Lodge.

13.5 mi.   Turnoff to the right leads to the only overnight parking
            for backpackers. The North Fork of Big Pine Creek Trail
            starts at the west end of the parking lot.

14.0 mi.   Glacier Lodge. The North Fork of Big Pine Creek Trail
            also starts at the end of Crocker Street, which is about a
            hundred yards to the north of Glacier Lodge. Although
            there is no overnight parking here, this start of the trail is
            more shady and scenic than the start from the overnight
            parking lot.

The northeast faces of Mt. Sill, Thunderbolt, North Palisade,
Starlight, and Polemonium are best reached by hiking the North
Fork of Big Pine Creek Trail.

You can start from either trailhead to reach the trail. From the
end of Crocker Street, the North Fork of Big Pine Creek Trail heads
northwest, soon crossing a large wooden bridge next to First Falls of
the North Fork of Big Pine Creek. The First Falls are about a quarter
of a mile from the end of Crocker Street. Once past First Falls, the
trail switchbacks up into a large basin.

Starting from the overnight parking area, the trail traverses
west across a slope covered with sage and gradually joins up with
the trail that leaves from Glacier Lodge. One and a half miles from
Glacier Lodge, or the overnight parking area, is Second Falls. The
trail switchbacks up and to the right (north) of Second Falls. The
North Fork of Big Pine Creek Trail continues up to the Big Pine
Lakes. Like the waterfalls along the trail, these lakes are named
First, Second, and Third Lakes.

After passing Third Lake and entering Sam Mack Meadow, a
sign is encountered that says "Glacier Trail". The Glacier Trail,
while at first obvious, fades amongst boulders and slabs and ends
between the southeast side of the Palisade Glacier and the northwest
side of Mt. Gayley. Mount Sill can be seen directly southwest of
Gayley connected by a steep, north-to-south running ridge. The
other peaks, Polemonium, North Palisade, Starlight, and
Thunderbolt can be seen in order to the northwest of Mt. Sill.

Mount Sill is readily approached from anywhere on the
Palisade Glacier (elevation 12,160 ft.) after hiking the Glacier Trail.
Small campsites, close to Sill's North Couloir are generally scarce.
Sites can be found in the moraine or in proximity to Mount Gayley.
This is a delicate alpine ecosystem and these bivy sites are used

quite frequently by many people. We have found tons of trash in this area and have spent a fair amount of time packing it out only to come back and find the area littered again. It is especially important to follow all wilderness ethics listed in Chapter 3 to prevent the area from being polluted through overuse.

Warmer, more comfortable campsites abound at Third and Second Lakes, or in the slightly cooler and exposed Sam Mack Meadow (elevation 11,400 ft.). Camping in either of these areas requires an earlier start and longer approach for climbing the North Couloir on Mount Sill.

10) North Couloir. Class 3

Although this route is somewhat exposed, the climbing is fairly straightforward. It is the easiest way to climb Mount Sill from the Palisade Glacier, and was first climbed by Walter Starr Jr., solo, on September 25, 1931.

The North Couloir Route on Mount Sill requires that the climber first surmount Glacier Notch, the low point in the ridge

Mount Sill from the north showing the route through Glacier Notch.

between Mt. Sill and Mt. Gayley. This can present a bit of a problem from the Palisade Glacier. The best route to gain the notch lies very close to the right (southwest) end of the ridge, just to the north of Mount Sill itself. The difficulty of Glacier Notch depends on the amount and type of snow present on that portion of the glacier. A dry and warm winter/spring can mean bergschrunds and ice at the notch. A good snowpack means firm early morning snow for hiking up and over the notch.

Climbers descending the North Couloir on Mount Sill.

The North Couloir (Route 10) of Mount Sill.

From Glacier Notch, head south towards the entrance of the couloir which is often snow-filled. The Swiss Arete will be on the left (east). Ascend the gully (the North Couloir itself) just right of the Swiss Arete for several hundred feet. At the top of the gully is a notch separating Mount Sill from a small tower to its north. Here, an exposed traverse (Class 3) up and right (west) leads across a steep chute. Climb up steep blocks on the opposite wall of the chute and angle south towards the summit until the northwest ridge is gained. From here, scramble eastward to the summit.

West Face Approach via Bishop Pass Trail:
     As with most of the Palisades, the west face of Mount Sill can
also be reached by traversing south after crossing Bishop Pass. The
following mileage chart and Map 7 describe how to get to the
starting point for the Bishop Pass Trail at South Lake:

Odometer Reading	Route Description at the Odometer Reading
0 mi.	Start at the corner of South Main, North Main, and West Line (Highway 168) in Bishop. Drive west on West Line.
14.9 mi.	Large sign describing South Lake Recreational Area. Turn left.
16.0 mi.	Jeffrey Campground on the left.
17.0 mi.	Habeggers R.V. Resort Park on the left.
17.8 mi.	Mountain Glen Walk-in Campground on the left.
19.0 mi.	Table Mountain Campsite on the left.
20.0 mi.	Willow Campground on the left.
20.8 mi.	Parchers General Store on the left.
21.8 mi.	The road forks. The right branch goes to South Lake and ends at the boat launching facility. Take left branch to the trailhead parking area.
22.0 mi.	Trailhead parking area.

     Starting from South Lake, the Bishop Pass Trail gradually
climbs into the high country while passing by many beautiful lakes.
Long Lake, and Bishop Lake are just a few of them. The hike up and
over Bishop Pass follows a well maintained trail. The trail crests at
Bishop Pass (elevation 12,000 ft.) just northwest of Mount Agassiz,
after about eight miles of hiking. From here, the trail descends to
the Middle Fork of the Kings River, where it joins the John Muir
Trail.
     At the crest of Bishop Pass, however, it is necessary to leave
the trail and traverse southeast across Dusy Basin, past the base of

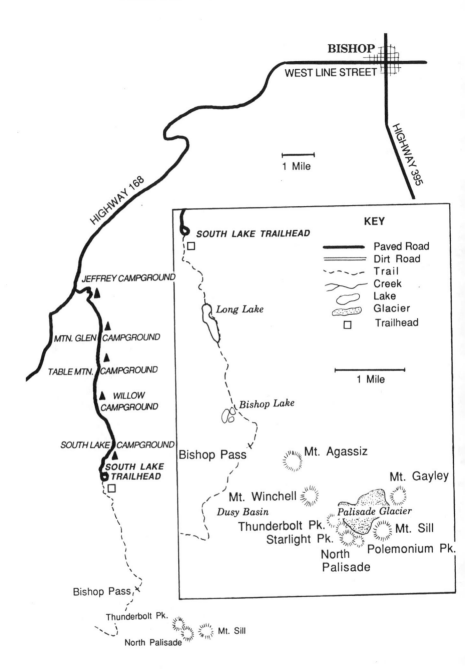

Map 7 — West faces of Mount Sill, Polemonium Peak, North Palisade, Starlight Peak, and Thunderbolt Peak

the southwestern faces of Mount Winchell and Mount Agassiz. Once past the faces, cross a small northeast-southwest ridge that extends perpendicularly from the main Palisade group. The easternmost (farthest left) notch in this ridge is Thunderbolt Pass (elevation 12,400 ft.).

Thunderbolt Pass is best surmounted close to the base of the Palisades. The first large chute to the east when you cross Thunderbolt Pass is the Southwest Chute of Thunderbolt Peak (Route 15). After crossing the pass and continuing south, you enter the Palisade Basin (elevation 11,600 ft.)

To the south, beyond Palisade Basin is Potluck Pass (elevation 12,140 ft.). There is excellent camping throughout Palisade Basin, however, this basin as well as Dusy Basin are extremely fragile ecosystems. Please be sure to pack out all trash and dispose of feces as mentioned in Chapter 3 (p. 12).

For the Southwest Chutes (Route 11) on the west face of Mount Sill, campsites are available on the south side of Potluck Pass. But, keep in mind that Potluck Pass is considered Class 3 and may be a little difficult to cross with a pack. We suggest camping in the Palisade Basin for climbing all the routes we have detailed for the fourteeners in the Palisades (Routes 11 through 15 on Mount Sill, Polemonium, North Palisade, Starlight, and Thunderbolt).

To get to Mount Sill's southwest chutes, cross Potluck Pass and head east towards the main crest of the Sierra Nevada. Mount Sill will soon come into view. Continue east on a rough trail and then turn left (north) up a steep cliff band (Class 1-2) that leads into a large southeast facing bowl known as the Polemonium Glacier Basin. Once above the cliff band, continue to the north towards the base of the Polemonium Glacier. You will soon see the southwest chutes above you. Behind you (to the west) will be Peak 13,962. To the left (northwest) will be the unobtrusive summit of Polemonium Peak. The Southwest Chutes (Route 11) heads straight up any of the central rock chutes from here.

11) Southwest Chutes. Class 2-3.

The numerous chutes that lie on the southwest side of Mount Sill provide the easiest way of achieving the summit. Indeed, the approach to the base of these chutes is far more arduous than the ascent itself.

Climb any of the chutes above the Polemonium Glacier to the summit. All the chutes are similar in nature, and most Class 3 rock can be avoided by traversing around into the next gully. A normal ascent takes about two hours.

Descent: Because Mount Sill can be climbed from two separate directions, each with their own 6-10 mile approach hike, we suggest that you descend your route of ascent. Descending the North Couloir (Route 10) requires careful down-climbing or several short rappels.

The west face of Mount Sill showing the southwest chutes.

15 *Polemonium Peak ~14,200 feet*

Although Polemonium was not considered to be a 14,000 foot peak for many years, the number of parties that make the extra effort to ascend the peak grows every year. The summit of this unobtrusive fourteener is as challenging as any in the Sierra Nevada. It requires not only rock climbing skill, but a good healthy set of nerves as well. The final summit block requires Class 4 climbing regardless of which side of the mountain is ascended.

On the south side of Polemonium lies the Polemonium Glacier which is the highest glacier in the Sierra Nevada.

CLIMBING POLEMONIUM PEAK

The easiest, but by no means quickest route to climb Polemonium Peak is via the Southeast Ridge (Route 12). By climbing Polemonium via the Southeast Ridge, you will pass below and to the west of the Southwest Chutes (Route 11) on Mount Sill. An ascent of Sill only takes a couple of hours and we recommend that the Southeast Ridge Route on Polemonium and the Southwest Chutes on Mount Sill be done in one day from a high camp in the Palisade Basin.

West Face Approach:

As with most of the Palisades, the west face of Polemonium Peak can be reached by traversing south after crossing Bishop Pass into Dusy Basin, and then continuing cross-country over Thunderbolt Pass into Palisade Basin. Follow the "West Face Approach via Bishop Pass Trail" directions along with Map 7 in the

Mount Sill Chapter (p. 56-58) to reach suggested campsites in the Palisade Basin.

12) Southeast Ridge. Class 3-4.

Polemonium Peak's southeast ridge joins with Mount Sill, and can be seen from the Palisade Glacier. You can get to the ridge from the Palisade Glacier, or the Polemonium Glacier Basin to the south. Gaining the ridge from the Palisade Glacier is much more challenging and involves Class 3 rock. The climb to gain the ridge from the south is Class 2.

The Southeast Ridge Route up Polemonium Peak can be reached two different ways. The first involves hiking from the Palisade Basin south towards Potluck Pass. Cross Potluck Pass and head east towards the main crest of the Sierra Nevada. Turn left (north) up a steep cliff band (Class 1-2) that leads into the Polemonium Glacier Basin. Hike northwest up the floor of the basin to the southeast tip of the glacier. Cross the glacier and continue to

This photo, taken from the summit of Mount Sill, shows the route up Polemonium Glacier to the Southeast Ridge and Polemonium Peak.
From L to R: *Peak 13,962, Polemonium Peak, the U-notch, and North Palisade.*

the highest point northwest, as shown below.

The second way to reach the Southeast Ridge Route involves first climbing the North Couloir Route (p. 53) on Mt. Sill from the Palisade Glacier. At the top of the North Couloir, instead of climbing southeast to the summit of Mt. Sill, climb northwest up and onto the southeast ridge leading to Polemonium Peak. Follow the ridge while avoiding the incredible chasms that slice the ridge and drop down to the Palisade Glacier. Continue on the ridge in a southwest direction to the high point which appears to be the summit of Polemonium.

The south summit of Polemonium as seen from the higher summit of Polemonium to the north.

After reaching what appears to be the high point, or south summit of Polemonium above the Polemonium Glacier, a deep gully to the northwest separates the end of the ridge from the actual summit. This steep gully falls away to the west, into Palisade Basin. Traverse north on steep rock, and drop down into the gully, for a hundred feet. Caution is essential as the rock here is phenomenally loose and there is a fair amount of exposure.

A traverse north over steep broken rock is necessary to reach the north summit of Polemonium Peak.

Another branch of the gully (the next branch to the north) will soon become visible, and leads back up to the right (north). Climb this and veer right near the top, gaining a steep face. From the top of the face, which provides a great view into the U-Notch, the summit will be obvious. The fine knife-blade ridge that must now be climbed is Class 4, but stunningly exposed. A rope is recommended.

Descent: Because the two routes we have described for Polemonium require separate approach hikes of 6-10 miles, it is best to descend your route of ascent.

The final steep rock to the north summit of Polemonium.

16 *North Palisade 14,242 feet*

North Palisade is the spectacular culmination of an incredible ridge called the Palisades. North Pal, as it is commonly known, is one of the most sought after summits in all California.

Joseph N. LeConte, James Hutchinson and J.K. Moffitt made the first ascent of North Palisade on July 25, 1903.

CLIMBING NORTH PALISADE

The easiest route to climb North Palisade is via the U-notch From The Southwest (Route 13). This route follows the original line of ascent, and is quite circuitous.

West Face Approach:

The west face of North Palisade can be reached by traversing south after crossing Bishop Pass. Once across Bishop Pass, many camping sites can be found in Dusy Basin. Hiking cross-country and then crossing Thunderbolt Pass will bring one into Palisade Basin which is the preferable location for starting routes on North Palisade. Adequate campsites can be found here. Both Dusy and Palisade Basin are extremely fragile ecosystems.

To get to the west face, follow the "West Face Approach via Bishop Pass Trial" directions along with Map 7 (p. 56-58) in the Mount Sill Chapter to reach suggested campsites in the Palisade Basin.

13) U-notch From The Southwest. Class 4.

This original ascent route has previously been called Class 3. However, we found certain sections of the couloir or gully section to contain rock steep enough to warrant a Class 4 rating. Still, it is the easiest route to the summit of North Pal.

From below the west face of North Palisade, three large white cliffs, approximately 500 feet tall, will be obvious on the lower right (southeastern) portion of the face. The gully that divides the two southernmost (right-hand) cliffs leads to the U-Notch, which is visible on the Palisade Crest above.

Enter the chute and climb steep, unforgiving talus to a huge flat slab, which is about halfway up the gully. It is impossible to miss this slab since it fills the entire chute. Here, the route becomes circuitous and route-finding requires some patience. Move to the left-hand (north) side of the gully. There is a steep wall on this side of the gully where a large open sloping ledge system can be seen above a vertical cliff. This cliff is often draining water, creating a very small waterfall on its uphill end.

Gaining the ledge system above is the key to the climb. From a point at the base of the vertical cliff, a very small, inconspicuous catwalk traverses down and left, across the cliff face itself. This traverse is a particularly strange key to the route up North Palisade because the ledge system traverses downward. Also, it is very narrow in many places. A rope may be a good idea here if the climbers are unsure of their abilities on steep ground. It is not uncommon to find cairns or "ducks" along the catwalk.

After reaching the lower end (west end) of the catwalk, move up and right (northeast), onto the large sloping ledge system. Climb up these ledges for several hundred feet, keeping well away from the edge of the precipice to the right. After surmounting a very small ridge that cuts the ledge system north to south, a narrow, steep, often snow-filled gully, will come into view. Ascend this gully by climbing either wet gravel or the snow that lies in it. Use the walls of the gully to surmount the two small roofs formed by boulders wedged in the gully. The rock here can be wet, making relatively easy climbing quite difficult.

At the head of the gully, a small ridge is surmounted, and the route turns north into a third, very broad, chute or bowl. Move left (north) into this south facing bowl and climb towards the high point to the north.

The west face of North Palisade showing the U-notch and Route 13.

Continue up the basin to gain the summit ridge. From here, the northeast face can be seen dropping away below. Turn west and continue climbing between the huge summit boulders until the summit platform is achieved.

It is strongly recommended that most parties bring a lightweight climbing rope and a small selection of nuts and carabiners. This route is easy to lose and even strong climbers have remarked on its wild exposure.

The catwalk of Route 13 to the summit of North Palisade.

<u>Descent</u>: Descending Route 13 is the easiest way down the mountain. The down-climb can be steep and slippery in places, especially in the second gully described, which is narrow and often snow-filled. Rappels may be necessary to descend this section. There are many solid rocks in this gully to which rappel anchors can be tied.

17 Starlight Peak
~14,200 feet

The summit of Starlight Peak offers the bold mountaineer the most exciting summit of all the peaks in the Palisades.

For many years, Starlight Peak was known as the Northwest Summit of North Palisade. It was considered nothing more than another lofty tower on the wildly serrated Sierra Crest. However, with the recent exploration of the huge buttresses, gullies, and aretes that lead to the spectacular summit pinnacle, the peak developed a reputation as well as a name of its own.

The first recorded ascent of Starlight was made on July 9, 1930 by Norman Clyde climbing solo.

CLIMBING STARLIGHT PEAK

The Northwest Chute on Starlight Peak is the most challenging route in this book. One should be adept at route-finding, Class 4 rock, and rappelling before attempting this peak. The Northwest Chute (Route 14) described here is the easiest and quickest route to climb Starlight Peak. The most popular route, however, involves traversing north from the summit of North Palisade and includes some Class 5 rock. The traverse south from Thunderbolt is not bad, but it too requires Class 5 climbing and can be time-consuming.

West Face Approach:

As with most of the Palisades, the west face of Starlight Peak can be reached by traversing south after crossing Bishop Pass into

Dusy Basin, and then continuing cross-country over Thunderbolt Pass into the Palisade Basin.

Follow the "West Face Approach via Bishop Pass Trail" directions along with Map 7 in the Mount Sill Chapter (p. 56-58) to reach suggested campsites in the Palisade Basin.

14) Northwest Chute. Class 4.

This route was first climbed on July 13, 1933, by James Wright and was actually a route to the summit of North Palisade. However, this route, with a small variation in the last few hundred feet, offers scramblers the easiest method of climbing Starlight Peak. Be aware that falling rock and ice may be encountered on this route.

Although the route is rated Class 4, it contains so much high-angle rock climbing that we suggest you bring a small rack of nuts, hexes, and a rope for an ascent. We have done this route many times (in addition to the other routes on Starlight) and we have found that rock climbing shoes can make this route and the summit pinnacle climb a little easier and more enjoyable.

There are two features that you must pay particular attention to while climbing and descending this route. The chute or gully that you enter at the start of the climb is known as the Lower Chute. After climbing for awhile you will traverse right (south) into the Upper Chute. This is the top half of the climb and like the Lower Chute contains sections of Class 4 climbing

To begin the Northwest Chute, enter the Lower Chute which is the third prominent chute or gully south of Thunderbolt Pass, and is also the first chute to the north of a large, fractured, triangular shaped buttress. This buttress is important because you will follow the gully that borders its north side and eventually climb south, through a notch behind the buttress, in order to gain the Upper Chute.

After entering the Lower Chute, make your way to its right (south) side and climb Class 4 rock. Follow the path of least resistance continuing up and right as the climbing grows progressively easier. As you come up close to the huge, blank triangular rock face that sits halfway up the mountain, look to the right (south) for a broken Class 3 shallow gully that leads to a sloping slab and notch.

Climb up this gully and cross the slab to the notch. The south side of this notch drops away dramatically into the lower portion of

Climber on the Northwest Chute (Route 14) on Starlight Peak. One hundred feet further, the climber will turn right (arrow) leaving the Lower Chute to enter the Upper Chute.

the Upper Chute. At this point you want to traverse east and downward across exposed, but secure Class 3 rock towards the center of the Upper Chute.

The Upper Chute is often filled with gravel and water from ice melt. Once in the center of this chute, move to its right side and climb steep rock for about two hundred feet. Above this, the angle becomes more gentle. Follow the gully, which is now composed of Class 2 and 3 climbing, gradually to the left (north).

After nearly 500 feet of scrambling, you will reach the top of the Upper Chute. The summit of Starlight is not visible at this point. Climb left up steeper and more difficult rock. At this point, less experienced mountaineers may wish to rope up since the next hundred feet encounters steep and sustained Class 4 rock.

As the rock steepens, move up and left. There are many variations in this final section and all are of about the same difficulty. Watch for rappel slings around you. Continue up this rock which is actually a ridge that drops west from Starlight's summit. At this point the top of the mountain may still be out of sight. The last few feet up to this ridge are exposed and strenuous. Once on top of this knife-blade ridge, the bottle-shaped summit of Starlight can finally be seen to the northeast.

Scramble over a huge, precariously balanced boulder, then across to the summit monolith.

The west face of Starlight Peak and North Palisade. The Northwest Chute (Route 14) on Starlight is shown.

Summit Pinnacle

There are two variations to climbing the summit pinnacle. One way is to free solo the south side of the pinnacle. Although exposed, it is no harder than Class 5.4.

The second way is to climb the south side with protection. This involves first mantling onto the south shoulder of the pinnacle and lassoing the summit with a rope or sling. The best way to lasso it is to tie some weight to the end of your rope or sling, throw it, and hope that it has enough momentum to come back around to you after circling the pinnacle. Tie your rope or sling around the

The summit of Starlight Peak can be quite exhilarating.

pinnacle. You now have an anchor that you can clip your rope to. Scramble up the south side of the pinnacle and place your rear end on the top. For a real adrenaline rush, try standing on top of the summit, while roped in of course. It feels like you are flying!

The bolt on the top of the summit pinnacle is rusty and should not be trusted. We don't know who put the bolt there but it was a bad idea. A runner or rope around the top of the horn more than adequately protects the climber for a rappel or from a fall.

Descent: The safest route of descent is Route 14, the Northwest Chute. Although it is possible to down-climb the entire route, there are three places where you may choose to rappel: 1) from the top of the knife-blade rib, just west of the summit, into the entrance of the Upper Chute, 2) halfway down the Upper Chute at the Class 4 section, and 3) at the bottom of the Lower Chute at the Class 4 section.

18 *Thunderbolt Peak 14,003 feet*

Thunderbolt Peak stands as the culmination of a one mile long portion of the Palisade Ridge that contains five peaks over fourteen thousand feet. Thunderbolt was the last fourteen thousand foot peak to be climbed in California, and it is one of the most spectacular.

On August 13, 1931, Bestor Robinson, Lewis F Clark, Glen Dawson, Jules Eichorn, Francis Farquhar, Robert L.M. Underhill and Norman Clyde, climbed Thunderbolt Peak for the first ascent.

CLIMBING THUNDERBOLT PEAK

The easiest and quickest route to climb Thunderbolt Peak is via the Southwest Chute (Route 15). This is a straightforward route to reach the summit monolith, and we thoroughly recommend it. We have also included descriptions of two different methods that can be used to climb the summit monolith.

West Face Approach:

As with most of the Palisades, the west face of Thunderbolt Peak can be reached by traversing south after crossing Bishop Pass into Dusy Basin, and then continuing cross-country over Thunderbolt Pass into Palisade Basin.

Follow the "West Face Approach via Bishop Pass Trail" directions, along with Map 7, in the Mount Sill Chapter (p. 56-58) to reach suggested campsites in the Palisade Basin.

15) Southwest Chute. Class 3.

Oscar Cook, Sylvia Kershaw, Mildred Jentsch, and Hunter and Isabella Morrison first descended this route on September 3, 1949. This is the most popular route on the mountain and probably the safest.

On the west face of Thunderbolt there is a very large and prominent chute which is the first chute directly south of Thunderbolt Pass. From Thunderbolt Pass, cross the talus and enter this first chute. Class 2 climbing brings you to a section of the chute that is boulder-choked. At this point, traverse right (south) out of the chute itself, and onto a low-angled face that circumnavigates the boulders. The chute then leads to a notch separating the northern summit monolith from the southern summit monolith.

The easiest way to reach the higher southern monolith is to hike a few feet south along the ridge from the notch. Look west for a sloping but steep face that contains horizontal cracks and handholds. Traverse west across this face (Class 3) and then upwards to the base of the south summit monolith.

The west face of Thunderbolt showing the Southwest Chute.

Climbing the final portion of the west face of the Thunderbolt summit monolith (Class 5.8).

Summit Monoliths

There are two summits on Thunderbolt Peak. Both are monoliths and are separated by a short distance. The South Monolith is the higher of the two, and contains the summit register. Since getting to the top of the South Monolith is what it's all about, we have presented information here that details how to go about this.

There are two known methods for climbing to the top of the higher South Monolith. The first, pioneered by the first ascentionists, is the best way to climb the monolith if you don't have a rope. Have a partner brace themselves against the east facing side of the block and then climb up and onto his or her shoulders. The move from here onto the rock, and the climb to the summit, requires a fair amount of balance, courage, and friction. Or to put it more bluntly, it involves hugging the rock for dear life while squirming up on your belly.

The second method, perhaps more dignified, involves throwing a rope over the summit block (east to west), traversing north and then west around the block, tying in, and then climbing the west face of the monolith while being belayed from the east. The difficulty is Class 5.8 and requires a good pair of climbing shoes. We recommend this route.

Descent: To descend the summit monolith, you can rappel down using one or both of the two bolts already on the summit (one holds the summit register down). If you don't trust the bolts, you can throw a runner or the rope over the southwest prow of the rock and rappel northeastward off of the block. We recommend using the bolts

Once off the monolith, the easiest and safest route to descend Thunderbolt Peak is via Southwest Chute (Route 15).   You can either hike northeast of the monolith for a few feet and rappel directly down into the notch, or climb down the Class 3 traverse.

19 White Mountain Peak 14,246 feet

Although not part of the extensive and physically dominating Sierra Nevada, White Mountain Peak commands the northern portion of the White Mountain Range and is the third highest peak in California.

CLIMBING WHITE MOUNTAIN PEAK

Since the parking area for the trailhead is at 12,000 feet elevation and the trail is basically a road to the top of White Mountain Peak, a quick hike to the summit is tempting. However, proper acclimatization is very important. Many experienced climbers have staggered into the Barcroft Facility complaining of severe headaches, nausea, dizziness, and shortness of breath. These are the classic signs of altitude sickness and should not be taken lightly. The Barcroft facility is available only in case of emergency. We strongly recommend that unless you are already acclimatized to at least 12,000 feet, you spend a night bivouacked at the parking area before proceeding to the summit. Another important point to remember is that there is no water available once you enter the Inyo National Forest. Therefore, you must carry your own water for the climb and descent of the peak. Sometimes there are some snowbanks on the north side of White Mountain Peak, but this depends on the previous year's snowfall. In addition, marmots, known for their penchant for radiator fluid, have been known to chew through rubber and brass radiator hoses here.

Approach to White Mountain Peak from the West:
The odometer chart and Map 8 describe the most popular and easiest way to the peak.

Odometer Reading	Route description at the Odometer Reading
0 mi.	At Big Pine (15.7 mi. south of Bishop on Highway 395), turn east onto Highway 168.
12.0 mi.	Continue on 168 past Cedar Flat Campground on the left. This campground requires advanced reservations.
12.6 mi.	Turn left onto White Mountain Road.
20.6 mi.	Continue past the Sierra View vista point which is on the left (west) and overlooks the spectacular Sierra Nevada and Owens Valley.
23.0 mi.	Turnoff for the Ancient Bristlecone Pine Forest.
23.6 mi.	The Schulman Grove Visitor Center turnoff. This is a recommended side-trip on the way to the White Mountain Peak. The oldest living bristlecone pine trees are located in the Schulman Grove.
23.7 mi.	White Mountain Road turns into dirt.
26.7 mi.	Continue north past the Silver Canyon/Wyman Canyon intersection. Silver Canyon heads left (west) towards the Owens Valley and is for 4x4 vehicles only. Wyman Road turns right and heads east, requires a 4x4 vehicle, and eventually connects with Highway 266.
32.7 mi.	Go straight (east)(right) towards Crooked Creek Station.
34.2 mi.	Patriarch Grove. Home of the largest bristlecone pine.
34.3 mi.	Continue past the Crooked Creek Station.
37.7 mi.	Parking area for the start of the South Face Route on White Mountain Peak.

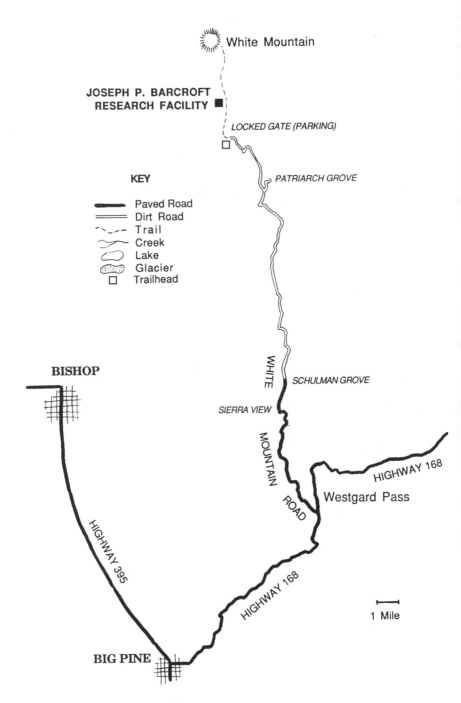

Map 8 — White Mountain Peak

White Mountain Peak as seen from the trail.

There are two signs at the end of White Mountain Road. One sign reminds climbers to: 1) please protect the delicate plants and animals that abound, 2) be aware that the hike is for foot traffic only, 3) be aware that there is no shelter at the summit, and 4) be wary of the severe storms that are possible on the peak. The other sign mentions that the Barcroft Facility is 2 miles from this point, and that the summit of White Mountain Peak is 7 miles from this parking area.

Approach to White Mountain Peak from the East:
Take the Highway 168 turnoff from Highway 266 whether you are driving south or west on Highway 266. Continue on Highway 168 west towards Westguard Pass. The White Mountain Road to White Mountain Peak is 0.8 miles from Westguard Pass. Turn right onto White Mountain Road and follow it as outlined in the approach from the west (p. 80).

16) <u>South Face. Class 1.</u>
This is the standard and easiest route to the summit, and is a 7 mile hike from the end of White Mountain Road to the summit. The trail is the service road that goes to the Barcroft Facility and continues up to the Summit Laboratory located on top of the peak. Since this road is wide and very obvious, many people have done hikes at night under a full moon. These can be cold but very enjoyable.

<u>Descent</u>: The South Face (Route 16) is the easiest and fastest descent from the summit of White Mountain Peak.

20 *Mount Shasta 14,162 feet*

Mount Shasta is a dormant volcano that belongs to the Cascade Range. Shasta is incredibly massive in bulk as well as height and dominates northern California as the single most prominent landmark for hundreds of miles.

The first recorded ascent of Shasta was made on August 14, 1854 by a Capt. E.D. Pearce, superintendent of the Yreka Water Company's sawmills, and eight other men. They ascended Avalanche Gulch.

Currently, there is a volunteer poop pack-out in effect for Avalanche Gulch. Ready made bags can be obtained at the Mt. Shasta Ranger Station, the 5th Season sporting goods shop, and at the Bunny Flat Trailhead.

CLIMBING MOUNT SHASTA

The easiest and most popular route on Mount Shasta is the Avalanche Gulch (Route 17) on the southwest side of the mountain. This route is considered Class 3.

Approach to the Southwest Side of Mount Shasta:

This is the most popular side of the mountain for climbers attempting the summit of Mount Shasta. Most of the starting points for the Avalanche Gulch Route begin at the end of the Everitt Memorial Highway. The two main starting points are, Bunny Flat and Sand Flat. The following mileage chart and Map 9 (p. 85) explain how to get to these areas on the Everitt Memorial Highway:

Odometer Reading	Route Description at the Odometer Reading
0 mi.	Start at the corner of Lake St. and Mt. Shasta Blvd. Go northeast on Lake St.
0.6 mi.	Turn left on Everitt Memorial Highway.
4.9 mi.	Campground on the left.
9.4 mi.	Everitt Vista Point on the right.
10.5 mi.	First Sand Flat turnoff. Sign reads, "Sand Flat 1/2 mile, Horse Camp Trail 1 and 1/2 miles, Horse Camp 3 miles".
11.1 mi.	Second Sand Flat turnoff. Sign reads, "Sand Flat 1/2 mile, Horse Camp Trail 1 mile".
11.9 mi.	Bunny Flat parking area. Outhouse present.
13.8 mi.	Panther Meadows Campground.
14.5 mi.	Mt. Shasta Ski Bowl Trailhead parking area.

The Everitt Memorial Highway will curve up and around the south flank of Shasta, switch-backing numerous times before reaching the trailheads. There are two access points from which to start the climb of the peak. One is Bunny Flat, and the other is Sand Flat. Sand Flat (elevation 6,800 ft.) has good overnight camping areas that are secluded and perfect for camping next to your car. Bunny Flat (elevation 7,040 ft.) avoids the hill out of Sand Flat but lacks ample camping sites.

If Sand Flat is your destination, we suggest taking the second Sand Flat turnoff while driving up the highway. If your destination is Bunny Flat, continue along the road; it is on the left hand side. Overnight parking is available at Bunny Flat. At the end of the Everitt Memorial Highway is a parking lot and the Ski Bowl Trailhead. As of this writing, there is no overnight parking at this parking lot.

17) Avalanche Gulch. Class 3. 1 Day.

The hike to the Sierra Club Hut (elevation 7,920 ft.) at Horse Camp is longer from Sand Flat (due to a 250 foot hill) than it is from

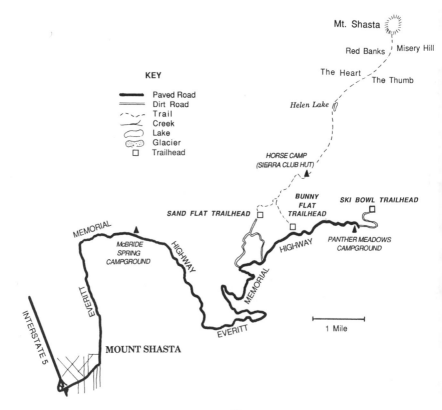

Map 9 — Mount Shasta

Bunny Flat. This hut, built in 1922, and supervised by a care taker, is open all year round to anyone who wants to use it. Some of the purest water in California is found in a spring next to this hut.

From the hut, the climb is roughly 4.1 miles but it involves an elevation gain of more than six thousand feet. A stone pathway known as the Olberman Causeway leads northeast from the hut towards the mountain. This pathway was built by and named after the first inhabitant of the Sierra Club Hut, J.M. (Mac) Olberman.

Follow the causeway since it eventually turns into the trail. The trail will curve to the left (northwest) ascending talus slopes to eventually gain a small plateau or shelf. Here you will find Helen Lake (elevation 10,400 ft.). The lake is very small and may often be frozen or covered with snow. The rock bench around Helen Lake is a good area for spending the night en route to the peak.

The southwest face of Shasta showing the Avalanche Gulch Route.
From L to R: *The Heart, Misery Hill, Red Banks, the Thumb.*

The area beyond Helen Lake involves a 2,000 foot high snowfield. This is the most difficult part of the climb, and also the most dangerous.

Beyond Helen Lake you will want to stay generally to the right (east) side of Avalanche Gulch. As its name implies, avalanches frequent this area from early to late summer. Most avalanches seem to originate from the Heart and the Red Banks which lie to the northwest and north respectively. It's a good idea to keep your eyes on these two formations at all times. You can usually see or hear these rock avalanches long before they become a threat.

Continue up Avalanche Gulch and ascend the 2,000 foot snowfield that leads to the right (southeast) of the Red Banks. You want to reach the saddle between the Red Banks and the Thumb which is a large gendarme on Sargents Ridge. If a bergschrund at the top of the snowfield is present and blocks further progress, then it is necessary to hike northwest up the southeast slope of the Red Banks. This variation of the normal route ascends loose, red, pebbly rock to the left of the snowfield and to the right of the Red Banks couloirs. At the worst it is loose Class 3.

Normally you can hike up the snow to gain the saddle between the Red Banks and the Thumb. Once at the saddle, continue northwest along the top of the Red Banks towards a prominent hill to the north. This hill is called Misery Hill and it is well named if you are feeling tired. The top of Misery Hill is the summit plateau. Directly north is a point of rock. This is the summit and it is usually climbed via a sandy slope that faces west. Just before you start up the slope to the summit, you can see the volcano's fumaroles to the left. There are many variations to this standard and very popular route.

Descent: The easiest descent from the summit of Mount Shasta is via the ascent route, Avalanche Gulch (Route 17).

The summit snowfield on Mount Shasta. The summit is on the right.

GLOSSARY

Because many of the route descriptions in this guide book use terms that hikers may not be familiar with, we decided to give a brief explanation of some of the terms that you might run into while reading this guide.

ARETE- A sharp ridge or edge usually present where two rock faces meet. A rock rib that separates two gullies.

BERGSCHRUND- A deep crack in the ice across the upper portions of a glacier.

BUTTRESS- A large, generally flat, portion of rock that stands out from the wall behind it.

CHIMNEY- A steep, narrow, chute or cleft with parallel rock walls.

CHUTE- A steep, well worn gully where debris often funnels down from the mountain.

COL- A high pass through a ridge.

COULOIR- A steep chute or gorge in the side of a mountain which does have, or is likely to have ice or snow.

CRACK- A parallel sided fracture in a rock, varying from the width of a hair to several feet.

DIHEDRAL- A crack or corner where two faces meet. Dihedrals are also known as "open books" due to their resemblance to a book that is open in the middle.

EXPOSURE- A term used to describe the vertical or steep nature of the location or terrain you are climbing on. For example, an exposed traverse might mean moving across relatively easy rock that is above a great vertical drop where a fall would probably cause serious or fatal injury.

FACE- A steep side of a mountain (generally steeper than 40 degrees).

GENDARME- A rock tower that makes up part of a ridge. They can vary in height from ten feet, to a hundred feet tall.

GULLY- A broad, generally low-angle depression that runs vertically down the side of the mountain.

KIOSK- A Forest Service trailhead marker in the shape of a bulletin board with an A-frame roof.

MASSIF- A group of high summits that are clustered together so closely that they are often considered all part of one mountain.

MORAINE- A enormous pile of gravel that has been scraped into place by a glacier, and often forms ridges, hills, and small valleys on its own.

PASS- An obvious cleft or break in a ridge where it is possible to cross.

PITCH- The division of a climb into segments limited to one rope length. A climbing rope is usually 165 feet long, therefore two pitches of Class 4 climbing would be approximately 330 feet.

PROW- The leading edge or face of a buttress or bulge that extends outward from the main portion of a wall, ridge, or mountain.

RIDGE- A high, usually long divide that protrudes from a peak. A ridge is also the joining point for two separate faces.

SLAB- A face on a mountain that is low-angled (generally less than 40 degrees).

SLOPE- A very low-angled face of a mountain.

SUMMIT- The highest point on a mountain.

TALUS SLOPE- Gravel, rocks, and boulders that have fallen from a mountain and compose a slope below the peak.

TARN- A small, high mountain lake usually light blue or green due to glacial silt.

WALL- A steep portion of a mountain that generally has fewer features than a face.